Dr. Aufrecht's

Pocket Guide to Critical Thinking

Dr. Monica G. Aufrecht, PhD

Edition 1.1

ISBN-10: 1492233919
ISBN-13: 978-1492233916

Table of Contents

POCKET GUIDE

Part I

This book is divided into three parts. **Part I** lays the groundwork, and is crucial for understanding the rest of the book.

Part II presents the heart of critical thinking, since it tells you about the two key questions one needs to ask about any argument. I suggest taking notes on Part II.

Part III provides numerous examples. It can be read in any order and perused at your leisure.

1. The Importance of Reasoning

What is so critical about thinking?

You don't believe everything you read or hear. Why?

The modern world is full of politicians, advertisers, spouses, roommates, and co-workers trying to convince you that they are right. Advertisers try to convince you their product is right for you. Politicians try to make you think they have the solutions. Pundits sound like they have all the answers.

Too often, these messages seems convincing, even when you know what they are saying is not true. We often feel that something is amiss in the message, but it can be hard to say exactly what is wrong.

In this book on Critical Thinking, I present techniques for understanding the logic behind these statements and conversations. I offer you the bare bones to get you started decoding these messages.

With these techniques, you will have a language to turn that "funny feeling" into an explanation. You will be able to explain to yourself and to others what is wrong with these messages (or what is right). Using this language, specifically: you will be able to identify and explain if the *arguments* being presented to you are *valid* or *sound*, and why.

2.   What it means to be "Critical"

There is a good reason for reasoning.

Scottish philosopher David Hume once argued that we should not believe in miracles. The concern, he said, is not that miracles don't happen. Maybe they do. However, he argued, we should not accept them without very *solid* evidence, and he believed that such evidence was lacking.

Whether the evidence for these miracles is strong or not is a matter of some debate, but our topic here is not miracles. Rather, this book is based on Hume's principle that **even if something is true, we should wait until we have been given good evidence for it before we accept it as true** (or as probably true).

To be clear, this does not mean we must wait until all the evidence is in before we act. Sometimes we need to act on incomplete or risky information. It also does not mean we take the other extreme, and consider everything we read or hear as false. That would be equally rash. Rather, the goal is to hold ourselves in a state of open question, until we get enough evidence, and we can clearly see how the evidence supports the ideas we are considering. Sometimes we never have enough evidence to know for sure, and then we must learn to live with uncertainty.

This principle forms the basis of modern logic and critical thinking. Thus, in this guide we do not explore whether a claim **is** true or false. Rather, we explore whether we have **good reasons** to think a claim is true or false.

3. Terminology

Be precise in your precision.

If you want to know whether to accept what someone is telling you, you need to understand what they are saying.

I am going to introduce you to some very powerful and complex concepts, and we need to be able to talk about them. Philosophers could have made up new words for these concepts, and in some cases they have, but for the most part, we will be reusing familiar words. So I ask you to set aside your current understanding of the following words, and to treat them as brand new words in a fancy new language.

These words include the following, all of which are defined in the glossary at the end of the book, along with many other new words:

1. argument
2. statement
3. premise
4. conclusion
5. evidence
6. valid
7. sound
8. weak
9. strong
10. cogent
11. fallacy
12. conditional
13. or
14. deduction

4.   Argument

Am not. Are too.

The first redefinition is **argument**. In everyday English, an argument is a messy, emotional event with lots of anger, yelling, and possibly blood. We do not mean any of that. To logicians, an argument is a beautiful thing, a piece of art that we strive to perfect. And it is the heart of Critical Thinking. In this book I teach you how to evaluate arguments. So here is our first definition:

An *argument* is: a series of **statements**, some of which are **premises**, and one of which is the **conclusion**.

Of course, this definition is not much help until we clarify the rest of the keywords in it:

A **statement** is a sentence that can be either true or false (i.e., has "truth value").

A **premise** is any statement that is used to try to convince us that the conclusion is true.

The **conclusion** is the statement that the arguer is trying to convince us is true.

For example, here are three arguments:

> I left the cookies on the table but now they are gone. *(premise)*
> If the cookies are gone, then someone ate them. *(premise)*
> If someone ate them, then someone has been here. *(premise)*
> Someone has been here. *(conclusion)*

> Organic food reduces pollution in the waterways. *(premise)*
> Reducing pollution is good for the environment. *(premise)*
> Organic food is good for the environment. *(conclusion)*

It is raining. *(premise)*
You should bring an umbrella. *(conclusion)*

The key here is that if we want to challenge someone's argument, we must challenge the premises, not the conclusion! We must look at the evidence presented, otherwise we are just **begging the question**. All of the tools in this book will be aimed at analyzing premises.

So the back and forth of "I am not." "You are, too!" may be an argument in the everyday sense, but does not qualify as an argument in our technical sense. Arguments must present premises, or what is more commonly called evidence.

5. Evidence

The first step is to sort out evidence from the other sorts of sentences people use. People often use **commands, exclamations,** and **questions**.

However, **only statements can be premises or conclusions because only statements have truth value. That means only statements present evidence that we can evaluate**. Examples of statements are:

1. It is raining.
2. Cats are mammals.
3. Sherlock Homes is a detective.

Commands are often used in trying to convince others, but as we will see, have no bearing on reasoning. They cannot be premises or conclusions. E.g.:

- Vote for me.
- Buy this car, you'll love it.
- Don't eat animals.

Questions, rhetorical or otherwise, are also often used to make a point and win an argument, but they do not present evidence, either. It is not even always clear what the questioner means to say. E.g.:

- Are you better off now than four years ago?
- Should we clean up the river?
- Was that a mistake?

For practice recognizing statements, consider the following sentences:

"Buses always run on time."
"If you don't leave now, you will miss the bus."
"Don't you think it is time to go now?"
"Go!"

Only the first two sentences are **statements**. The first statement is false (buses are often late), and the second statement might be true or false – we do not have enough information because we do not have the full context (who is leaving, how far is the bus stop...). But because these sentences can be true or can be false, they are both statements and so both of these sentences are eligible to be premises or conclusions.

However, the last two sentences are not statements. Rather they are a question and a command. It makes no sense to say "Go!" is true, or to say it is false, which means "Go!" cannot be a premise or a conclusion.

Sometimes when people ask questions or give commends they are trying to make hidden or implied claims. For instance, perhaps the command "Go!" is intended to mean "You should go now if you want to catch the bus" (which is a statement that might be true or false).

It is possible, though tricky, to **rationally reconstruct** someone else's argument. That means you take their commands, questions, and exclamations, turn them into statements that can serve as premises and conclusions, and then add any implied premises. This is tricky because you might be wrong about what someone else intended to say. However, it is important to give someone the benefit of the doubt and rationally reconstruct their argument, if you can. This is especially important if you don't want to lose all your friends after reading this book. They might also have hidden valuable insights that you could learn from, even if they are not as skilled at Critical Thinking as you are.

So, for instance, we can rationally reconstruct one of the questions above. We make the implied statements explicit:

> Premise 1. You are worse off than you were four years ago.
> Premise 2. If you are worse off than you were four years ago, then you should not re-elect the same president.
> Conclusion. You should not re-elect the same president.

The premises now present reasons that we can engage with and ask questions about. (*Are the premises true? Am I worse off? If so, does that mean we should change course?*) In contrast, commands, questions, and other non-statements do not provide reasons to convince anyone of anything.

Already you have learned a powerful lesson of Critical Thinking: Premises must be statements that provide evidence, and the conclusion must make a clear assertion.

6. Normative or Descriptive

Normally these quotes are descriptive.

Statements can be divided into two types: **descriptive** and **normative**.

Descriptive statements describe the way things <u>are</u>.

1. It is raining right now.
2. Cats are four-legged animals.
3. Your shoes are under the bed.

Normative statements describe the way things <u>should be</u>. "Should" is based on moral, evaluative, or aesthetic considerations. E.g.:

1. You should not kill.
2. Eating animals is wrong.

Many people mistakenly believe that normative statements are mere opinion, and thus cannot be used as evidence. However, if your opinion is supported by good reasons, then there is nothing "mere" about it! **Some of our most important beliefs are normative, and we have rational arguments for believing them to be true.** E.g.:

Premise 1. "It is wrong to hurt people." *(normative)*
Premise 2. "Discrimination hurts people." *(descriptive)*
Conclusion: "Discrimination is wrong." *(normative)*

Note that in order to have a normative conclusion, you must generally have at least one normative premise. 19th century ethicist John Stuart Mill, for instance, suggested a normative premise that he thought everyone would agree to ("Pain and suffering is bad, in and of itself.") He used it to build his ethical arguments.

7. Simple vs. Compound Statements

One and one is true.

You can combine **simple statements** to make **compound statements**. You combine them using these four **logical connectives**:

- and
- not
- or
- if/then

"Or" has two meanings. Inclusive "or" means one or the other or both. Exclusive "or" means one or the other, but not both. In this book, we mean "or" in the inclusive sense.

Simple statements are statements that do not have any logical connectives in them. Compound statements are made up of simple statements *and* logical connectives.

To make the structure of a sentence easier to see, sometimes we represent a simple statement with a variable such as capital letter X, Y, Z, or P, Q, R. I know that looks really *mathy*, but it really is just a simple replacement. For example:

Simple statements:
X: I am hungry.
Y: I forgot my lunch.
Z: I was running late.
P: Someone distracted me.

Compound Statements:

I am hungry **and** I forgot my lunch. (X **and** Y).

If I forgot my lunch, **then** I was running late **or** someone distracted me. (**If** Y, **then** Z **or** P).

I am **not** hungry. (**Not** X).

The logical connective if/then is so powerful and so misunderstood that it gets a name and a whole chapter.

8. Conditional Statements

If I were omniscient, then I would have all the answers.

Some simple statements depend on other simple statements. These most commonly take the form of *"If X then Y"* and are called **conditional statements.** E.g.:

1.   If it rains, then you will get wet.
2.   If Flipper is a dolphin, then Flipper is a mammal.
3.   If Juan eats a peanut, then he may die.

The simple statement after the "if" is called the **antecedent** (E.g. "It rains.")

The simple statement after the "then" is called the **consequent** (E.g. "You will get wet.").

Although these compound statements have two parts, the compound statement *as a whole* is a perfectly good premise in an argument. This is obvious in the following example:

> Premise 1. If Rover is a dog, then Rover wags his tail.
> Premise 2. Rover is a dog.
> Conclusion. Roger wags his tail.

Conditional statements have some very strange properties. Here are the most important:

A. You cannot switch the Antecedent and Consequent

> If the Titanic was retired from a long career, then the Titanic is not running today. *(true)*
> If the Titanic is not running today, then the Titanic was retired from a long career. *(false)*

B. Except when you can

In some rare cases you *can* switch the antecedent and the consequent:

If a person is alive, then that person is breathing. *(true)*
If a person is breathing, then that person is alive. *(true)*

In this case, the switch is possible because breathing is both necessary for a person to be alive, and generally if someone is breathing, that is sufficient to indicate they are alive (ignoring brain death, here). But in the previous example, being retired after a long career would be enough to stop the Titanic from running, but it is not the only way.

Many, many invalid arguments result from people switching the antecedent and the consequent when they aren't supposed to. These bad arguments are tricky to spot, so we will learn tools for spotting them later in the book.

C. To make a conditional false…

If the antecedent is true but the consequent is false, then the whole conditional is false.

"If Abraham Lincoln was murdered, then he is alive today." *(false)*

This may at first seem odd, but will make sense when you remember that the conditional "If X, then Y" is claiming that X is enough to make Y happen. So if X happens, and Y doesn't happen, then the conditional claim is false. Here is another example of a false conditional:

"If you care about the environment, then you should stop emitting carbon dioxide entirely." *(false)*
(Remember, humans exhale carbon dioxide, so the consequent is false!)

D. Otherwise it is true

If the antecedent is false, then the whole conditional is true.
(This is really weird!)

"If faster-than-light travel is possible, then I am Captain Kirk." *(true!)*

"If the Cubs win the World Series, I will eat my shirt."
  (true, if it is impossible for the Cubs to win.)

Conditional statements are so counter-intuitive, and so important, that we could go on and on about them. For now, the important thing to remember is that **when you are looking at a conditional statement, you cannot consider the antecedent or consequent in isolation; rather you have to consider the entire conditional statement.**

9. Finding Arguments

The truth is out there. The evidence is right here.

In every day life, arguments are typically presented as a jumbled paragraph, and so it is difficult to separate the premises from the conclusion. Sometimes, some of the premises are implied, rather than stated explicitly. This type of argument is called an **enthymeme**. E.g.:

> *"Oat Nut Crunch is high in fiber, and full of essential vitamins, so it is a great part of a healthy breakfast."*

Breaking this down, we can separate out the premises and conclusion:

> Premise 1. Oat Nut Crunch contains fiber and vitamins.
> Premise 2. Fiber is healthy. *(implied)*
> Premise 3. Vitamins are healthy. *(implied)*
> Conclusion. Oat Nut Crunch is healthy.

Enthymemes are very common, and very tricky. Often the implicit premise is the controversial premise:

> *"Genetically engineered food is Frankenfood. They are putting fish genes in tomatoes! This has to stop."*

> Premise 1. Genetically engineered food is not natural.
> Premise 2. Any food that is not natural is not safe. *(implied)*
> Premise 3. Any food that is not safe must be stopped. *(implied)*
> Conclusion. Genetically engineered food has to be stopped.

Implied Premise 2 is the controversial one. By not stating it explicitly, the speaker can sound more convincing, without actually addressing the issue. This is how two sides can talk past each other without resolving their issues:

> *"People are starving throughout the world. For this reason, genetically engineered food is desperately needed."*

Premise 1. People need (safe) food.
Premise 2. Genetically engineered food is safe. *(implied)*
Conclusion. Genetically engineered food is needed.

Again, the unstated premise is controversial, making this a weak argument. A stronger argument would explicitly address the controversy, and provide reasons to think that GMOs are safe.

Beware! Not all paragraphs contain arguments:

Unemployment rose again this month, to a new high of 9.8%. The Senate introduced a bill to extend unemployment benefits for 99 weeks, and the House is expecting to vote on this bill later this week.

I really wish you would wash your clothes. The washing machine is right there. Here is some soap.

Genetically Modified Organisms (GMO) are organisms that have had their genes modified. Genes can be deleted, changed, or even added from other genes, such as adding fish genes to tomato genes. GMOs are used in both research and agriculture.

10. Deduction and Induction

Elementary, my dear reader.

There are two kinds of arguments: ***deductive*** and ***inductive***. In Critical Thinking, these terms differ in meaning from the common uses in both mathematics and Sherlock Holmes stories.

In ***deductive*** arguments, the conclusion follows directly from the premises, adhering to a set of proscribed logical rules described later in this book.

In ***inductive*** arguments, the conclusion goes beyond the premises; if the premises support the conclusion, and the premises are true, then the conclusion is probably true, but not necessarily always true; it is speculative.

Below is an example of a **deductive** argument:

P1. All horses are mammals.
P2. All mammals are animals.
C. All horses are animals.
(From here onward, to save space and make the arguments easier to read, we'll abbreviate the premises as P1, P2, ... and abbreviate the Conclusion to 'C')

If the two premises are true, then there is no doubt that the conclusion is also true. Even without knowing the rules of logic, common sense makes this "feel" correct.

Below is a second **deductive** argument:

P1. If Mars is Earth-like, then people live there.
P2. There are no people living on Mars.
C. Mars is not Earth-like.

The argument may be more difficult to understand, but like the previous example, the conclusion logically follows from the premises: if the two premises were true, then the conclusion would have to be true (even though the first premise is not actually true!). If this doesn't make sense yet, don't worry. We will discuss it in detail in Part II.

In comparison, below are two examples of **inductive** arguments:

> P1. Most people who study do well in class.
> P2. Jill studies.
> C. Jill probably will do well in class.

> P1. Cigarette smoke often causes lung cancer.
> P2. Jack smokes cigarettes.
> C. Jack probably will develop lung cancer.

In these examples, as in all inductive arguments, it is improbable that the premises could be true while the conclusion is false, but it is possible.

We have just learned several new concepts that help us recognize arguments, and whether evidence is being presented at all. Next we will figure out if the evidence really supports the conclusion.

Part II

Okay, hold onto your hats. Everything in the book so far is leading up to the next three chapters, and the rest of the book is just reflection on them. So, I recommend you grab a pen and write down these three core concepts:

1. An argument is **valid** when it would be impossible for the premises to be true and the conclusion false at the same time.

2. An argument is **sound** when the argument is valid *and* all of its premises are true.

3. Valid arguments can be "good" or "bad," but sound arguments are always "good." When an argument is **sound**, you can be **certain** that its conclusion is true!

I know this gets confusing fast. So keep these sentences in front of you. Refer to them often while you read the rest of the book. If you can master the concepts of valid and sound, then you can master Critical Thinking.

11. Logic

Logic is wreath of pretty flowers...

When analyzing an argument, we ask two questions:

1. **Are the premises true?**

2. **Do the premises logically support the conclusion?**

If the answer to both of these questions is *yes,* then bingo! You have a good argument, and so you have good reasons to believe the conclusion.

However, if the answer to either question is *no,* then you should not be convinced. The conclusion might still be true! But the evidence presented is insufficient. Keep looking for better evidence, or, if you really think the conclusion might be false, look for evidence that shows it is false.

So, how can you find the answers to the first question? As I tell my students, that is what your other classes are for. To figure out whether the premises of an argument are true, use your education, your life experience, experts you trust, and, of course, further arguments.

For the second question, to figure out whether the premises support the conclusion, that is what the rest of the book is for. Use logic! There are many logical tools to help answer this question, including truth tables and proofs of formal logic. We will focus on **forms.** But before we introduce forms, we need to discuss what it means for a premise to "logically support" a conclusion.

12. Valid Arguments

Neither volume nor repetition makes an argument more valid.

Suppose you and a friend want to take a trip and you are trying to decide whether to visit the Grand Canyon or Berlin. Your friend says, "Hey, look, we should go to the Grand Canyon. The flights to Tokyo are really expensive, and we are trying to save money." We can rationally reconstruct this argument:

Invalid:
P1. Flights to Tokyo are really expensive.
P2. We should not take flights that are expensive.
C. We should go the Grand Canyon.

Your friend has offered two premises, but they are unrelated to the conclusion. They do not logically support it. When the premises do not support the conclusion, the argument is called **invalid**.

But suppose your friend offers these arguments instead, "Flights to Berlin are expensive, and we are trying to save money. Let's not go to Berlin, and let's drive to the Grand Canyon instead." There are actually two conclusions hidden in here, so we **rationally reconstruct** this as two separate arguments:

Valid:
P1. Flights to Berlin are expensive.
P2. We should not take flights that are expensive.
C. We should not fly to Berlin.

Valid:
P1. We should not fly to Berlin.
P2. We should fly to Berlin or we should go to the Grand Canyon.
C. We should go to the Grand Canyon.

In each of these arguments, the premises logically support the conclusion. That is to say, it would be impossible for these premises to be true and the conclusion false at the same time. Such arguments are **valid.**

Validity is about the *logical relationship* between the premises and the conclusion. We are not saying anything about whether the premises are actually true (at least, not yet). To determine validity, we __*pretend*__ the premises are true, then ask ourselves, "Must the conclusion be true, as well?" If so, the argument is valid. If not, it is invalid.

A valid argument is a good start, but it isn't enough. It means that if the premises *were* true, then the conclusion would be true, too. But validity does not tell us whether the premises are *in fact* true. It turns out that a valid argument might have one or more false premises! In that case, we have not been given good reasons to accept the conclusion.

Valid (but unconvincing):
P1. If you can walk from New York to Berlin, then you can afford to go to Berlin after all.
P1. You can walk from New York to Berlin.
C. You can afford to go to Berlin.

We have now learned enough that we can explain the funny feelings around some arguments. One way an argument can seem good is if the premises lead to or support the conclusion. But if the premises turn out to be false, then it still isn't a good argument.

Other times, that "funny feeling" comes about when the argument being presented is invalid. Sometimes invalidity is obvious:

Invalid:
P1. Winter is cold. *(true)*
P2. It snows in the winter. *(true)*
C. Snow is white. *(true, but still invalid)*

Other times, invalidity is very subtle:

Invalid:
P1. If a TV show is bad, then it gets cancelled. *(true?)*
P2. *Friends* got cancelled. *(true)*
C. Therefore, *Friends* is a bad TV show. *(false)*

Invalid:
P1. All superheroes are good guys. *(true)*
P2. Superman is a good guy. *(true)*
C. Therefore, Superman is a superhero. *(true, but still invalid)*

In the above three cases, all the premises are true, but the conclusions do not logically follow from the premises. So if you find yourself nodding along to a salesman, thinking, "Yes, it is true I need a new car, and yes, it is true that interests rates are low right now, but, wait, why do I need to buy a car from *you*??", then she is probably telling you an invalid argument with true premises.

Of course, when an argument is *invalid* and has false premises, then it should be rejected entirely!

Invalid:
P1. Cows lay eggs. *(false)*
P2. Eggs taste great for breakfast. *(true)*
C. You should buy this cow. *(false)*

So we see that this definition of "valid" has some strange implications.

A. True Conclusions

An argument can be invalid even when the conclusion is true. In the example above, it is true that Superman is a superhero, but the premises do not actually give us evidence for that claim. Plenty of people are "good guys" without being superheroes. This point is especially important to remember when, say, fighting for political causes. If your friends are presenting bad arguments for good causes, you can help them by replacing their invalid arguments with valid ones for the same conclusion. For instance, suppose your friend is trying to convince people to become vegetarians:

Invalid:
P1. If you have a pet, then you love animals.
P2. You have a pet.
C.   You shouldn't eat animals.

Even if the premises are true *and* the conclusion is true, the above premises do not logically support the conclusion. It is possible, in some imaginary universe, for these premises to be true and yet the conclusion to be false. So, instead, if you want to *convince* people to believe the conclusion, you need to start with premises that support the conclusion:

Valid:
P1. If you love animals, then you don't want them to suffer.
P2. If you don't want them to suffer, then you shouldn't eat them.
P3. You love animals.
C.   You shouldn't eat animals.

B. False Premises

Remember, the premises do not need to be true for an argument to be valid (or invalid). The definition of valid requires us to ***pretend*** that the premises are true. If doing that would force the conclusion to be true, then the argument is valid. It does not require the premises to actually be true. For example, the following are both valid arguments:

Valid:
P1. Everything with wings can fly. *(false)*
P2. All pigs have wings. *(false)*
C.   All pigs can fly. *(false)*

Valid:

P1. An Ostrich is a bird. *(true)*

P2. All birds can fly. *(false)*

C. Ostriches can fly. *(false)*

In both cases, at least one premise is false, and in these cases, the conclusion is also false. However, if those premises were true, then the conclusion would also be true.

Given all the bizarre side effects, this may seem an odd definition for *valid*, but as you will see it turns out to be enormously powerful. And if this definition bothers you, as it does many of my students when they first learn it, don't worry. Remember that these arguments about pigs flying still aren't good arguments, because **being valid is a good start, but it is not enough.** We also need all the premises to be true. Only then do you know the conclusion must be true.

13. Sound Arguments

It sounds like valid arguments are not the end of the story.

We have finally arrived at our goal: a good argument. A **sound** argument is a **valid** argument where all the premises are actually true.

Sound (i.e. Valid with True premises):
P1. All bats can fly.
P2. The flying fox is a type of bat.
C. All flying foxes can fly.

The argument above is both **valid** and **sound**. The following arguments are **valid** but **unsound**:

Valid but Unsound:
P1. Everything with wings can fly. *(false)*
P2. All pigs have wings. *(false)*
C. All pigs can fly. *(false)*

Valid but Unsound:
P1. An Ostrich is a bird. *(true)*
P2. All birds can fly. *(false)*
C. Ostriches can fly. *(false)*

So we see that that uneasy feeling also arises from arguments that are valid but not sound: the premises would support the conclusion if they were true, but the premises are actually false.

With this structure in mind, look at advertisements, read the comments section of articles, and listen to your friends. You'll now start to notice when their arguments are valid, but where one of their premises is false or controversial. You will also notice where their premises do not support the conclusion. You will see that the world is full of arguments that are unsound.

Part III

The rest of the book is a long list of forms. Forms are templates for arguments. The more forms you learn, the better. I picked a combination of common forms and very tricky forms to include in this book. But even if you learn just one form, you'll be doing great. You will start seeing that form everywhere, and now you will be able to critique it (in the case of invalid forms or fallacies), or accept it without fear (in the case of valid forms).

14. Forms

Forms follow logical functions.

Now we know that good deductive arguments need to be valid and have true premises. But how can you tell if an argument is valid?

Earlier we introduced the idea of simple and compound statements. We also used variables such as X and P to represent simple statements. This allows us to create forms.

Forms are structures of arguments. If an argument fits a valid form, then the argument is valid. Invalid forms are almost as simple. If an argument does not fit into a valid form, but it does fit into an invalid form, then it is invalid.

We can look at the form of an argument and figure out if it is valid without even knowing what the argument is about! This is very useful when debates get heated and we are worried about emotional bias, or when we just plain don't understand what someone is telling us. (Yes, in those cases, we should have everyone "clarify terms" whenever possible, i.e. clearly define the words they are using, but it is actually possible to show someone's argument is unconvincing without even knowing what they are saying. Logic is cool!)

For example, the following arguments:

    P1. If it is raining, then the sidewalks are wet.
    P2. It is raining.
    C. Therefore, the sidewalks are wet. *(valid)*

    P1. If paradigms are incommensurable, then scientific development is noncumulative.
    P2. Paradigms are incommensurable.
    C. Therefore, scientific development is noncumulative. *(valid)*

Both become:

    P1. If P, then Q.

    P2. P

    C. Q (valid)

    Note that P and Q are the traditional letters used as stand-ins for statements in logic, just as x and y are the traditional letters used for unknowns in Algebra.

Remember our example about superheroes?

    P1. All superheroes are good guys. *(true)*

    P2. Superman is a good guy. *(true)*

    C. Therefore, Superman is a superhero. *(true but invalid)*

This has the form :

    P1. All As are Bs.

    P2. X is a B.

    C. X is an A. *(invalid)*

This argument might not strike you as invalid right away. To check it, you can replace "Superman" with another name, keeping the same form:

    P1. All superheroes are good guys. *(true)*

    P2. Mickey Mouse is a good guy. *(true)*

    C. Therefore, Mickey Mouse is a superhero. *(false and invalid)*

Now it is more obvious that the argument is invalid. The conclusion is false even while the premises are true.

Why does the conclusion not follow? I'll explain this shortly. But even just looking at the logical form, you should agree that these premises do not lead to the conclusion, so this argument is invalid. Booya!

In the following chapters, we will learn four valid forms so common and so important that they have names. We will also learn the two trickiest, and most common, invalid forms.

15. Valid: Modus Ponens

A form so important we speak of it in Latin.

Being able to name a complicated idea is incredibly important. It helps us recognize the idea, talk about it, and use it ourselves. And if you want to sound really cool, you name the idea in Latin.

In the logical form of **Modus Ponens**, there are two premises. One premise is a conditional statement (i.e. if..then), and the other premise matches the antecedent (i.e. the "if"). The conclusion matches the consequent (i.e. the "then").

Modus Ponens:

P1. If P then Q.

P2. P.

C. Q. *(valid)*

Note: the symbols P and Q are used here to focus on the form, rather than the specific statements. The letters P and Q are traditional for logic, just as x and y are traditional within Algebra.

Below is an example of this form, both in written and ***rationally reconstructed*** form:

I already told everyone that if no one helps me with the picnic this weekend, then I'm going to cancel it. And no one has been helping me, so that's it. I'm canceling the picnic.

Here the statement "No one helps me with the picnic." is P. and the statement "I'm going to cancel the picnic." is Q.

P1. If no one helps me with the picnic (P), then I'm going to cancel the picnic (Q).

P2. No one helps me with the picnic. (P)

C. I'm going to cancel the picnic. (Q) *(valid, Modus Ponens)*

35

16. Valid: Modus Tollens

Once speaking Latin, it is hard to stop.

In the logical form of **Modus Tollens** you also have two premises. One premise is a conditional. The other premise claims the consequent is not true. The conclusion asserts that the antecedent is not true, either.

Once again without the jargon: given an *if...then,* and the *then* is not true, then the *if* is also not true.

> **Modus Tollens:**
> P1. If P, then Q.
> P2. Q is not true.
> C.   P is not true. *(valid)*

Unlike Modus Ponens, Modus Tollens is not so obviously valid.

The reasoning goes like this: pretend P were true. Then according to the first premise, Q would also be true. But according to the second premise Q is not true. Since according to that first premise, we can't have P true and Q not true, then the only possibility is that P is not in fact true. That matches the conclusion.

The *assumption* within this and the other forms is the rule that that P must either be true or false. Given the two premises and that rule, there is only one logical conclusion.

Below are two examples:

> *If you are going to catch a train, then you have to get to the station on time. But you are late. So you will miss the train.*

> P1. If you are going to catch a train, then you have to get to the station on time.
> P2. You will not get to the station on time.
> C.   You will not catch the train. *(valid, Modus Tollens)*

I'm delighted that it is sunny on today's trip, but I cannot find my sunglasses anywhere. I could have sworn I put them in the suitcase, but I must not have brought them with me after all.

P1. If I had packed my sunglasses, I would have them.
P2. I do not have my sunglasses.
C.   I did not pack them. *(valid, Modus Tollens)*

17. Valid: Hypothetical Syllogism

If you give a mouse a cookie...

In the logical form of **Hypothetical Syllogism** you draw a conditional conclusion from two conditional premises.

> **Hypothetical Syllogism:**
> P1. If P then Q.
> P2. If Q then R.
> C. If P then R. *(valid)*

It likely reminds you of the transitive property in mathematics, *if A = B and B = C then A = C.* Like Modus Ponens, this fits our common sense, every day logic.

Below is an example:

> *With our new product, we expect to double our revenues, which will in turn triple our profits.*

> P1. If we build the new product, we'll double our revenues.
> P2. If we double our revenues, we'll triple our profits.
> C. If we build the new product, we'll triple our profits. *(valid, HS)*

18. Valid: Disjunctive Syllogism

Easier to understand than to pronounce.

The logical form of **Disjunctive Syllogism** requires a new kind of compound statement, one in which two simple statements are connected by an "or." Such a compound statement is true if either simple statement is true. An "or" statement is a called a **disjunction** and each simple statement is called a **disjunct**. For example:

> *We can go to the beach today, **or** we could catch a movie (or both).*

In a **Disjunctive Syllogism**, one premise is a disjunction. The other premise says one of the disjuncts is not true. The conclusion is that the remaining disjunct must be true.

Disjunctive Syllogism:
P1. P or Q.
P2. Not Q.
C. P *(valid)*
Note: "Not Q" is shorthand for "Q is not true"

If this is not obvious, let's look at the reasoning. The first premise states that either P or Q (or both) are true. The second premise states that Q is not true. If P were also not true, then the statement "P or Q" would be false. So P must be true.

Below is an example, which should make this form quite obvious:

> *Either Kamal or Liz need to attend to event. Kamal is out of town that day, so Liz needs to attend.*

Disjunctive Syllogism:
P1. Kamal needs to attend or Liz needs to attend.
P2. Kamal cannot attend.
C. Liz needs to attend. *(valid)*

Remember, we have just determined the argument is valid, but we do not know if it is sound. That is, we still do not know if the premises are in fact true. If we want to accept the conclusion as true, we would need to find out if Kamal really is busy, or if Kamal and Liz are our only options.

But suppose you are presented with an argument and you have no way of knowing if its premises are true. In some cases, you can still declare the argument unsound anyway. You can do this if the argument is invalid. So next up: invalid forms.

19. Invalid: Affirming the Consequent

Wolves in sheep's clothing.

There are two invalid forms that are so tricky, and so common, that they have names. Being able to identify invalid forms is one of the most powerful skills you learn in this book. Be careful how you talk about it, though, so you don't offend people. And be prepared to get into long debates with people who don't believe you that their arguments are invalid.

The first invalid form is ***Affirming the Consequent***.

Affirming the Consequent looks a lot like Modus Ponens, but the conclusion does not follow from the premises.

Affirming the Consequent:
P1. If P then Q.
P2. Q.
C.   P. *(invalid, Really!!!)*

To reiterate, this is <u>not</u> logically correct. It is a common mistake of logic. For example:

Affirming the Consequent:
P1. If you grew up in France, then you speak French. (true)
P2. You speak French.
C.   You grew up in France. *(invalid)*

Growing up in France is a sufficient condition for knowing French, but not the only way to learn French. French is spoken in over a dozen countries, and many other people learn it as a foreign language in school. Thus not all people who speak fluent French grew up in France.

The logical reasoning behind this mistake is simple. Sure, the conclusion might actually be true. But the premises do not lead with certainty to the conclusion.

However, this mistake is so common because people often mix up the antecedent and the consequent in their minds. Someone might *think they said*:

P1. If you speak French, then you grew up in France. *(false)*
P2. You speak French.
C. You grew up in France. *(valid, Modus Ponens, unsound)*

Now the argument is valid! But the first premise is clearly false, making this argument unsound.

Listen carefully and you will hear the invalid Affirming the Consequent form used in many arguments. Remember the form and you will be able to explain the odd feeling when an argument feels valid, but is not.

20. Invalid: Denying the Antecedent

These are not the premises you are looking for.

The other mistake common enough to deserve a name is **Denying the Antecedent**. This invalid form often reminds people of Modus Tollens, but the conclusion does not follow from the premises.

Denying the Antecedent:
P1. If P then Q.
P2. Not P.
C. Not Q. *(invalid)*
Note: "Not P" is shorthand for "P is not true"

To reiterate, this is <u>not</u> logically correct. It is a common mistake of logic. For example:

Denying the Antecedent:
P1. If humans lived on Mars, we'd have pictures of Mars.
P2. Humans do not live on Mars.
C. We have no pictures of Mars. *(invalid)*

This argument is invalid. Remember, a valid argument is one where the premises would guarantee the conclusion. Yet here the premises are true, but the conclusion is false! We *do* have pictures of Mars; they were taken by robots, not people, despite no human ever living there. So the premises, even though they are true, give us no reason to accept the conclusion.

The logical reasoning behind this mistake is that in the statement "If P then Q", if P is not true, we cannot conclude anything about Q. It may be true and it may not be true. That statement doesn't tell us either way, and thus we can not conclude Q, nor can we conclude "Not Q." Given only "If P then Q" and "Not P," nothing further can be logically concluded.

Here are two more examples of the invalid Denying the Antecedent form:

P: The Titanic is on fire.
Q: The passengers should get on a lifeboat.

Denying the Antecedent:
P1. If Titanic is on fire, then the passengers should get on a lifeboat.
P2. The Titanic is not on fire.
C. The passengers should not get on a lifeboat. *(invalid, DA)*

and

P: I am a dog.
Q: I am warm blooded.

Denying the Antecedent:
P1. If I were a dog, I would be warm blooded. *(true)*
P2. I am not a dog. *(true)*
C. I am not warm blooded. *(false and invalid, DA)*

This argument has true premises and yet a false conclusion, so it is clearly invalid.

Yet even if the conclusion were true, an argument of this form would still be invalid. That is, the premises would not be good evidence for the conclusion.

Even presidential candidates can make invalid arguments:

> *"The proof of whether a strategy is working or not is what the price is that you're paying at the pump. If you're paying less than you paid a year or two ago, then the strategy is working. But you're paying more. When the president took office, the price of gasoline here in Nassau County was about $1.86 a gallon. Now it's $4.00 a gallon."*
> -- Mitt Romney, U.S. Presidential Debates, 2012

Denying the Antecedent
P1. If gas prices go down, then Obama's plan is succeeding.
P2. But gas prices went up.
C. Obama's plan failed. *(invalid)*

Here, it looks like Romney meant the first premise to say, "If Obama's plan is succeeding, then gas prices would go down." That would have made this argument a valid Modus Ponens!

In this case, someone might agree with the stated premise one, but not with the unspoken premise that Romney *intended*. Thus they might find themselves agreeing with the stated premises, and then having a fishy feeling that something isn't right, since in fact the stated premises do not lead to the conclusion. (Incidentally, Barack Obama responded to the *intended* premise, not the stated one.)

If you can't for the life of you figure out why this argument is invalid, maybe it is because you agree with both the stated first premise *and* the unstated (but intended) premise, in which the antecedent and consequent are switched.

So note that much confusion can arise when people mistakenly switch the antecedent and the consequent!

21. Examples of Logical Forms

To help you grasp the logical forms, below are a series of examples. (The answers appear on the next page).

A.

> P1. If using your cellphone while driving were illegal, then you shouldn't do it.
> P2. It's not illegal.
> C. It's OK to use your cellphone when driving.

B.

> P1. If a large asteroid were to hit the earth, all life would be destroyed.
> P2. If all life were destroyed, it would be terrible.
> C. If a large asteroid were to hit the earth, it would be terrible.

C.

> P1. If the dog barks, the baby wakes up.
> P2. The baby woke up.
> C. The dog barked.

D.

> P1. We should not fly to Berlin.
> P2. We should fly to Berlin or we should go to the Grand Canyon.
> C. We should go to the Grand Canyon.

E.

> P1. If the autopsychological basis is innate, then intersubjective objectivity is possible.
> P2. The autopsychological basis is not innate.
> C. Intersubjective objectivity is not possible.

F.

    P1. If you don't get in the car now, we won't catch the next ferry.

    P2. If we don't catch the next ferry, we will be late to the wedding.

    C. If you don't get in the car now, we will be late to the wedding.

G.

    P1. If someone is a superhero, then they are a good guy.

    P2. Mickey Mouse is a good guy.

    C. Mickey Mouse is a superhero.

H.

    P1. If someone is a superhero, then they are a good guy.

    P2. Mickey Mouse is not a good guy.

    C. Mickey Mouse is a not superhero.

I.

    P1. If you didn't eat your peas, you cannot have dessert.

    P2. You didn't eat your peas.

    C. You cannot have dessert.

J.

    P1. If you eat your peas, you can have dessert.

    P2. You didn't eat your peas.

    C. You cannot have dessert.

K.

    P1. If you can have dessert, then you eat your peas.

    P2. You didn't eat your peas.

    C. You cannot have dessert.

Answer key:

A. Invalid – Denying the Antecedent

B. Valid - Hypothetical Syllogism

C. Invalid - Affirming the Consequent, because the first premise claims that the dog barking is enough to wake the baby, but it doesn't claim that it is the only way to wake the baby.

D. Valid – Disjunctive Syllogism

E. What does this mean? Who knows! But it is invalid – Denying the Antecedent

F. Valid – Hypothetical Syllogism

G. Invalid - Affirming the Consequent

H. Valid – Modus Tollens. Note that P2 false, so even though the conclusion is true, this argument is unsound.

I. Valid – Modus Ponens

J. Invalid!! Denying the Antecedent. No wonder kids get so confused. Here peas are offered as a sufficient way to get dessert, but not necessarily the only way.

K. Valid – Modus Tollens. This sounds very awkward, but P1 is the same as saying: "You can have dessert **only if** you eat your peas." (See "only if" in the glossary.)

22. Inductive Arguments

As we have seen, sound arguments are utterly convincing. In sound arguments, the premises logically support the conclusion (that is, the argument is valid), and the premises are true. Sound arguments guarantee a true conclusion.

So why don't we see sound arguments everywhere? It turns out that it is really hard to be that certain about anything (or at least about anything interesting). Here is a sound argument:

P1. Mother's Day is on a Sunday.
P2. Monday comes after Sunday.
C. The day after Mother's Day is a Monday.
   (Valid, true premises, and boring)

Valid arguments with false premises are easier to come by:

P1. If you want women to love you, you should buy this deodorant.
P2. You want women to love you.
C. You should buy this deodorant. *(valid, unsound)*

It is a valid Modus Ponens! But premise 1 is false, so this argument is unsound, and therefore not very convincing.

Both of these are examples of deductive arguments. But much more common are **inductive arguments** – arguments where the premises ditch certainty, and instead give us good reason to think the conclusion is only *probably* true. These arguments are **strong** when the premises likely support the conclusion, and **weak** when they do not. If, by added bonus, the premises are also *true,* then a strong argument becomes **cogent.** Cogent is to inductive arguments what sound is to deductive arguments: as good as it gets.

One big difference between deductive and inductive arguments is that validity for deductive arguments is cut and dry. An argument is either valid or invalid. However, for inductive arguments, strength is a matter of degree, and of opinion, so an argument that one person finds strong, another might find weak. This makes it very tricky to analyze inductive arguments. Thus, forms can help you identify and clarify points of disagreement.

23. Inductive forms

Arguments you can believe in.

Here are four common **strong** Inductive Argument Forms:

A. Strong: Arguments from Analogy

> P1. X is similar to Y.
> P2. Y has property Z.
> C. X has property Z. *(strong)*

For example:

> P1. Parenting is big responsibility, just like driving a car.
> P2. If you want to drive a car, you have to get a license.
> C. Parents should also have to get a license. *(strong?)*

B. Strong: Generalization

> P1. All/most **observed** Xs have property Y.
> C. All/most Xs probably have property Y. *(strong)*

For example:

> P1. All observed humans have been mortal.
> C. All humans are probably mortal. *(strong)*

C. Strong: Argument from Authority:

> Person X said Y.
> Person X is qualified to speak on Y.
> :. Y is probably true. *(strong)*
> *Note: the :. Is shorthand for "therefore"*

For example:

> P1. Professor Gonzalez said that the house you are considering buying is on an earthquake fault line.
> P2. Professor Gonzalez is a geologist with 20 years of experience in this area.
> C. Thus, the house is probably on a fault line. *(strong)*

D. Strong: Reductio Ad Absurdum (RAA)

This argument comes in a few versions. In one version, the premises lead to the conclusion with absolute certainty, so that makes this version deductive. It is really a fancy version of Modus Tollens: If P, then Q, but Q can't possible be true, so P must be false, too.

Deductive version

> X would lead to Y.
> Y is a contradiction.
> :. X is false. *(valid)*

> P1. My client was on surveillance video at the mall at 9:02am, but the jewels were stolen across town at 9:02am. If my client stole the jewels, then he would have to be in two places at once.
> P2. It is impossible to be in two places at once.
> C. Thus, my client did not steal the jewels. *(valid)*

However, a similar argument is often used to reject proposals of action, among other things. In this other case, the premises strongly suggest the conclusion is true, but do not guarantee it, so this version is inductive.

Inductive version

> X would lead to Y.
> Y is unacceptable.
> :. X should be rejected. *(strong)*

> P1. If you buy a house on a fault line, it could be destroyed in an earthquake.
> P2. It would be terrible if your house were destroyed in an earthquake.
> C. Thus, you should not buy a house that is on a fault line. *(strong)*

Note: This following is not an appropriate use of RAA:

> P1. If a large asteroid were to hit the earth, all life would be destroyed.
> P2. It would be terrible if all life were destroyed.
> C. Thus, an asteroid will not hit the earth. *(weak!)*

Just because you don't want something to happen, that alone doesn't mean it won't happen. But it does mean you should take steps to prevent it, if you can. So a more appropriate conclusion would be:

> C. We should fund asteroid research to stop asteroids from hitting the Earth.

24. Fallacies

Please ignore the man behind the curtain.

For each of the strong inductive forms we have seen, there is a weak counterpart. These are called **fallacies;** they look convincing, and so tend to trick people (sometimes even the arguer!).

A. Weak Analogy

When two ideas or two things are similar but not identical, you cannot assume the properties of one are inherent in the other.

P1. X is similar to Y.
P2. Y has property Z.
C. X has property Z, too.

This argument form is weak when X is not similar to Y in the *relevant way.* For example:

P1. The best professional soccer players are paid millions of dollars.
P2. I scored five goals at recess today.
C. So I should be paid millions of dollars too. *(weak)*

B. Hasty Generalization

The observed properties of an idea or object are incorrectly assumed to apply to all similar ideas or objects. This form is weak when you observe only a few objects, or unusual objects.

P1. This observed X has property Y.
C. All Xs have property Y. *(weak!!)*

For example:

> *I used rubbing alcohol every day my whole pregnancy and my baby is fine, so there is no problem for you to use it when you are pregnant.* *(weak, you cannot generalize from one person here)*

C. Unqualified Authority

The person providing the evidence is not qualified to speak on that topic, and thus while he or she states the evidence as true, it may not be true. E.g.:

> My three year old nephew told me:
> P1. The people on the moon make glow sticks.
> P2. The moon people glow their glow sticks every night.
> C.   Moonlight comes from glow sticks. *(valid, but not sound)*

D. Slippery Slope

The conclusion depends on an unlikely chain of possibilities. It is like a Reductio Ad Absurdum, but here the absurd outcome is unlikely to occur.

> P1. If A then occasionally B.
> P2. If B then sometimes C.
> P3. If C then unlikely, but possibly D.
> P4. A.
> C.   D. *(weak)*

For example:

> P1. If there is no rain for a week, then there might be a forest fire.
> P2. If there is a forest fire, it may get out of control.
> P3. If the forest fire gets out of control, my house, twenty miles from the forest, may burn down.
> P4. It has not rained for a week.
> C.   My house will burn down. *(weak)*

Note, some people reject arguments of this form because the outcome is so *bad.* However, that does not determine whether the argument is weak or strong! Rather, the question we should be asking is: Is the outcome likely or unlikely? If it is unlikely, then we do not need to worry about it. If the bad outcome is *likely,* however, then we should take action to stop the first step down the slope.

E. Ad hominem attack

Attacking the person presenting the argument, rather than any of the premises within the argument.

Person A
P1. If X then Y.
P2. X.
C.   Y *(valid)*

Person B
P1. You are ignorant

This may sound crazy, but is a very common form of attack in politics, in business, and in life in general. E.g.:

Person A
P1. Global warming is the greatest threat to humanity.
P2. If we do not act soon, it will hit a tipping point.
C.   We need to act now. *(strong RAA)*

Person B
P1. Person A has a big house that emits a lot of carbon. So we do not need to act. *(weak)*

F. Straw Man

Attacking a weak, misleading "straw" version of the opponent's argument.

Person A makes an argument, perhaps something like:

P1. If X then Y.

P2. X

C. Y *(valid)*

Person B

(Changing the argument) "Person A said, e.g.:

P1. If X then Y.

P2. W

C. Z *(invalid)*

This too is common in politics, business, etc., e.g.:

Person A

P1. If we are to get less turnover amongst our workers, then we must pay them a living wage.

P2. We need less turnover.

P3. We can afford to pay the workers.

C. We should pay the workers a living wage. *(valid)*

Person B

"Person A says

P1. If we pay our workers $50/hr., they will be happier.

P2. I agree that happier workers have less turnover.

C. We should pay workers enough to all live in mansions."

Person B then continues, "Clearly that is ridiculously expensive, so we should not pay our workers whatever Person A wants us to." *(weak)*

Straw Man arguments are very hard to identify, unless you happen to know what Person A said, and then they are easy to spot (and infuriating!). **The take away lesson here is that if one person is describing another person's argument to you, and that argument sounds crazy, go check it out for yourself before dismissing it.**

G. Missing the Point

The premises lead to one conclusion, but the arguer draws a different, unrelated conclusion.

P1. If X then Y.
P2. X
C. Z *(invalid)*

In politics and business this is often done on purpose, to avoid answering the question that has been asked. Elsewhere, this fallacy occurs when the argument is informal in nature, and the premises are not clearly laid out and thus difficult to logically parse. E.g.:

P1. Enron was a public company.
P2. Enron broke the law, and deceived its customers.
P3. Enron went bankrupt.
C. To prevent another Enron we need to regulate private companies. (*weak*)

H. Red Herring

This fallacy is similar to Missing the Point, but involves the premises, rather than the conclusion. In a **Red Herring**, the arguer changes the subject by introducing a true premise that has nothing logically to do with the conclusion. But since the premise is true, the listener often finds herself agreeing with the arguer.

Person A
P1. If X then Y
P2. X
C. Y *(valid)*

Person B
P1. Z *(weak)*
C. Not Y

For example:

Person A
P1. Germany has doubled its solar installations last year.
P2. Solar is good for the environment.
C. We should increase our solar installations. *(valid)*

Person B
P3. But we fought Germany in WWI and WWII.
C. So we should not use solar power.

Red Herrings are tricky because the distracting premise is so tempting: it is true, and often important, but almost always irrelevant. Just because someone is telling you something true, that doesn't mean they are giving you evidence for their conclusion. Remember, their evidence has to be *relevant!*

I. Begging the Question

The conclusion is just a restatement of the premises. No new reasons are given.

> P1. X
> C. X *(valid)*

This seems too simple to happen in real life, but it is actually one of the most common pitfalls of informal arguments. E.g.:

> *We need a toll on the bridge, because that way the drivers will pay each time they use the bridge.*

> P1. We need drivers to pay a toll when they use the bridge.
> C. Therefore, we need a toll on the bridge. *(valid, but unconvincing)*

Interestingly, begging the question is logically valid, so technically not a fallacy. Still, you haven't been presented with any evidence for the claim, and so there is no reason to be convinced of the conclusion.

J. Equivocation

When there is a word in the premises that shows up in the conclusion, but with a different meaning in the two statements.

> P1. If X then Y_1
> P2. X
> C. Y_2 *(invalid)*

This can be very subtle, especially when a word has multiple meanings, which is not uncommon in English. E.g.:

The average Walmart salary is $14/hr., so I don't know why the average worker is complaining about making minimum wage.

P1. The average (mean) salary at Walmart is $14/hr.
   Note: The mean includes the salaries of management.
P2. $14/hr. is well above minimum wage.
C. Therefore, the average (median) worker has nothing to complain about. *(invalid!)*

Note: More than half of the Walmart staff is paid minimum wage, thus the median paid worker (and in fact most of the workers) are paid well below $14/hr. *(weak)*

Equivocations can also be found in jokes, where the meaning within a sentence changes from the premise to the conclusion. E.g. this anonymous joke I found on the internet:

A wife asks her husband, a computer programmer; "Could you please go to the store for me and buy one carton of milk, and if they have eggs, get 6!"

A short time later the husband comes back with 6 cartons of milk. The wife asks him, "Why the hell did you buy 6 cartons of milk?" He replied, "They had eggs."

K. Appeal to Ignorance

Given no evidence that a premise is true, it is assumed to be false. E.g.:

No live aliens have been seen in public, on television, or film, thus there are no such things as aliens. (weak)

As Donald Rumsfeld rightly said, lack of evidence is not evidence of lack.

25. Examples of Fallacies

To help you grasp the logical forms, below are more examples.

A.

> *WaiterDude: Tipping is unfair! I've been a waiter for 2 years now, and the waitresses all get higher tips than me. People tip based on looks, not service.*

B.

> *CatLover: @Dude, you are just saying that because you want more money. Better service gets better tips. Period.*

C.

> *Albert214: Well, @CatLover, it is true you can't generalize from one person's experience. But a recent study in <u>Waiter's Weekly</u> of 500 waiters shows that most customers don't actually tip based on service. In fact, the women in the study got higher tips on average than the men, even though independent observers rated their service quality as equal. So WaiterDude is right. Our current tipping system is unfair.*

D.

> *J34ml: @Albert214 Thanks for the link to the study. Interesting stuff. But the study doesn't mention race. Tipping may be sexist, but at least it isn't racist.*

E.

> *LongDays: The tipping system is fair. It is not racist or sexist. Waiters and waitresses both work hard for their money. In most states they get paid below minimum wage, and need tips in order to survive.*

F.

VoiceOfReason: Hi folks! I think we all agree that we want servers and customers to be treated fairly, don't you? Let's find a better system!

G.

HappyCamper: @LongDays says that waiting tables is the hardest job in the world, and so servers should get the highest salaries. But if we pay servers more, then it would be too expensive for anyone to go out to eat. All restaurants would go our of business, and all the servers would be fired. We should leave things the way they are.

H.

BigTipper: I was watching the TV show Friends, the one where Rachel was a waitress, served a coffee, and received no tip. So @ Albert214's study is wrong. Good looking waitresses don't get tipped at all.

Answer key:

A. Weak – Hasty Generalization. We can not generalize to all servers based on the experiences of one server.

B. Weak – Ad Hominem attack. Even if WaiterDude does want more money, CatLover should respond to his argument, not his character or motivation. AND Weak – Begging the Question. WaiterDude's conclusion is "Tips are not based on service." CatLover simply restates the negation of the conclusion ("Tips are based on service") without giving any evidence, or properly addressing WaiterDude's (admittedly weak) argument.

C. Strong – Appeal to Qualified Authority AND Strong – Generalization

D. Weak – Appeal to Ignorance. We cannot conclude anything about race one way or the other. More information is needed.

E. Weak – Red Herring. Although LongDays makes good points, they are irrelevant to her conclusion ("the tipping system is not racist or sexist").

F. Um, this is a nice sentiment, but there is no argument here.

G. Weak – Straw Man. LongDays said that waiting tables is hard, not that it is the hardest job. And LongDays didn't actually say anything about how much waiters should be paid. HappyCamper is distorting what LongDays said and thereby creating a Straw Man argument. She then tries to knock it down, but with another weak argument – a Slippery Slope. It is unlikely that paying servers more would lead to the series of events as described. AND Weak – Missing the Point. The conclusion ("We should leave things the way they are") is not warranted by the argument given (even if it weren't weak). A more reasonable conclusion would be the pay servers a bit more, but not so much that restaurants go out of business.

H. Weak – Unqualified authority. A fictional TV show is not a good source of information about the reality of working in a restaurant. AND Weak – Hasty Generalization. The study is looking for trends, and one exception, fictional or not, does not disprove a trend.

26. Conclusion

Absence of evidence is not evidence of absence.

We started with the basic principle that we should not believe anything without evidence. I conclude with its corollary: we should not reject anything without evidence, either.

When my students encounter an argument with premises they know nothing about, they often conclude that the argument is unsound.

Consider the following argument:

P1. If God exists, then there is an afterlife.
P2. God exists.
C. So, there is an afterlife. *(valid, Modus Ponens)*

Many of my students have told me they simply do not know if the second premise is true, and so they reject the argument as unsound. However, **if you do not know whether the premises are true or false, *then you do not know whether the argument is sound*.**

Moreover, the tools in the book have shown that when you have a sound argument (a valid argument with true premises) then you have really good reason to believe the conclusion. The opposite is not true, though. If you have a unsound argument, then you have not learned anything new, nor have you lost anything. There might be better arguments out there for the same conclusion.

Consider these two unsound arguments:

"You should buy this car. It is blue and matches your eyes, and you should buy a car based on color." (valid, unsound)

"If Bill Gates won the lottery, then he would be rich. Bill Gates won the lottery, so he is rich." (valid, unsound)

Maybe you should buy this car, though not for the reasons given (the second premise is false), and Bill Gates certainly is rich, although as far as I know he never won the lottery.

So just because someone presents you with a bad argument, that is no reason to accept *or reject* their conclusion!

The uncomfortable lesson of critically thinking is that we must learn to live with uncertainty. If we do not have enough evidence, we must withhold judgment, gather more information, and then develop or adjust our beliefs based on new evidence as it comes in.

Sometimes we must even *act* with incomplete information, such as in urgent situations or if the risks of inaction are dire. But then it is better to acknowledge that we are uncertain and taking action anyway, than to pretend we know something for certain, when we do not. Acknowledging uncertainty allows us to make important corrections mid-action based on new information, when such corrections are necessary.

"When you know a thing, to hold that you know it; when you do not know a thing, to allow that you do not know it – this is knowledge."
                                                                  - Confucius.

APPENDIX

Warning: Use with Compassion!!

One student told me this story, "I asked my sister to baby-sit, and she responded with a Red Herring. I told her that, but she just looked at me blankly and left. I ended up staying home. Now she won't talk to me." Many people love to be right. This book will help you be right more often and will help you recognize when other people are wrong. But being right and winning arguments is not the point. A better goal is to find the truth together, as friends, lovers, communities, and as nations. Many students have come to me at the end of class, grateful for their new logical powers, but having lost all their friends. We humans are at our best when we connect with one another with compassion. Ultimately, critical thinking can help us solve our problems together, by helping us connect with each other and understand each other.

Further Reading:

Thinking critically / Critical Rationalism history

The Open Society and its Enemies by Karl Popper

Logic

Logicomix: An Epic Search for Truth by Apostolos Doxiades, Christos Papadimitriou

Goedel, Escher, Bach: An Eternal Golden Braid by Douglas Hofstadter

Language

Don't think of an Elephant: Know your values and frame the debate by George Lakoff

Words that work: It's not what you say, it's what people hear by Frank Luntz

Language Intelligence: Lessons on persuasion from Jesus, Shakespeare, Lincoln, and Lady Gaga by Joseph J Romm

Critical Thinking Textbooks

Introduction to Symbolic Logic by Patrick Hurley

The Art of Reasoning by David Kelley

Acknowledgements

Thank you to my incredible husband, who inspired me with his writing to follow suit, and who never stops pushing me to expand Critical Thinking beyond the halls of the Philosophy department, out into the wider world. You rock.

To my teachers and colleagues, Arthur Fine, S. Marc Cohen, Cass Weller, Ben Stenberg, Ben Almassi, Joe Ricci, Luke Hannah, and Stephanie Patridge; and to my students, who showed me the nuances of the subject. Thank you for all that you taught me, and all that we learned together.

About the Author

Dr. Monica Aufrecht is a Philosopher of Science, with a Ph.D. in Philosophy from the University of Washington. She has taught at Linfield College, Simon Fraser University, the University of Washington, and the Seattle Colleges.

In years past, she was a Research Fellow at the Max Planck Institute in Berlin, and a Graduate Fellow at the Simpson Center at the University of Washington.

Dr. Aufrecht's researches the ethics of science, climate change, and distributive justice, and above all else loves to teach Critical Thinking and Logic, which she holds to be the basis of civilization.

Glossary

Affirming the antecedent – Another terms for *Modus Ponens*, which is a valid argument form.

Affirming the consequent – An invalid argument form: If P, then Q. Q. Therefore P.

Antecedent – The "if" part of a conditional statement. The antecedent presents a sufficient condition that is enough to bring about the *consequent*. In the conditional "If Flipper is a dolphin, then Flipper is a mammal," the antecedent is "Flipper is a dolphin." There are many ways to be a mammal, but being a dolphin is sufficient for being a mammal.

Argument – A series of *statements*, some of which are *premises*, and one of which is the *conclusion*.

Begging the question – An argument in which the conclusion is just a restatement of the premises. No new reasons are given, so little or no evidence is presented. Note that sometimes people say something "begs the question" when they mean it "opens up more questions." That is not the same meaning we are using here.

Cogent – An inductive argument that is strong and has true premises. Cogent arguments are very good.

Command – A sentence that tells someone what to do. Not a statement. Cannot be a premise or a conclusion.

Compound statements – Statements made up of simple statements *and* logical connectives.

Conclusion – A statement that one is trying to convince you to believe.

Conditional – An "if..then" statement, such as "If Flipper is a dolphin, then Flipper is a mammal."

Consequent – The "then" part of a conditional statement. The consequent presents a necessary condition, something that is required for the *antecedent*. In the conditional "If Flipper is a dolphin, then Flipper is a mammal," the consequent is "Flipper is a mammal." It is impossible to be a dolphin without also being a mammal. Being a mammal is necessary in order to be a dolphin.

Deductive – Arguments where conclusion supposedly follows directly from the premises.

Denying the antecedent – An invalid argument form: If P, then Q. Not P. Therefore Not Q.

Denying the consequent – Another terms for *Modus Tollens*, which is a valid argument form.

Descriptive – Statements that describe the way things are.

Disjunct – The options being presented in an "or" sentence. For example, in the disjunction "Apples are green or red," the left hand-disjunct is "Apples are green" and the right-hand disjunct is "Apples are red."

Disjunction – An "or" sentence. Note that the English "or" has two meanings. The inclusive "or" means *one or the other or both*. Ex. "No food or drinks permitted." *The e*xclusive "or" means *one or the other, but not both*. Ex. "You may have soup or salad with that." In this book, we mean "or" in the inclusive sense.

Disjunctive Syllogism – A valid argument of the form: P or Q. Not P. Therefore, Q. The name means "an argument with two premises with an *or* statement."

Enthymeme – An argument where a premise or conclusion is implied. Sometimes the implied premise is obvious and trivially true. Consider the argument: "Kicking cats causes them pain, so you shouldn't kick cats." The missing premises is "Causing pain is bad." Sometimes the implied premise is controversial, and people don't even realize it is there. Then it is important to make it explicit so that it can be debated.

Exclamation – A sentence that expresses a feeling or makes a noise, such as "Ouch!" Not a statement. Cannot be a premise or a conclusion.

Evidence – A reason to believe something. The evidence might be strong or weak, true or false, convincing or unconvincing, but at least something is being presented in support of a conclusion.

Fallacy – Arguments that are weak or invalid. They often trick people, though not always intentionally. Many people use fallacies without intending to.

Hypothetical Syllogism – A valid argument of the form: If P, then Q. If Q, then R. Therefore, If P, then R. The name means "an argument with two premises and conditionals."

Inductive – Arguments where the conclusion goes beyond the premises, and the conclusion is probably true, but not necessarily always true; it is speculative.

Invalid – An argument is invalid when it is possible for the premises to be true and the conclusion false. The premises do not logically support the conclusion.

Logical Connective – A word that connects statements. This book includes the logical connectives: *and, or, if..then*, and *not*.

Modus Ponens – A valid argument of the form: If P, then Q. P. Therefore, Q. Latin, meaning "the Mode of Affirming."

Modus Tollens – A valid argument of the form: If P, then Q. Not Q. Therefore, not P. Latin, meaning, "the Mode of Denying."

Normative – Statements describe the way things should be.

Only if – Indicates the consequent of a conditional. "If Flipper is a dolphin, then Flipper is a mammal" is equivalent to "Flipper is a dolphin only if Flipper is a mammal." There is a big difference between "if" and "only if"! "If" indicates a sufficient condition, while "only if" indicates a necessary condition.

Or – The common English "or" has two meanings. The inclusive "or" means *one or the other or both.* Ex. "No food or drinks permitted." *The* exclusive "or" means *one or the other, but not both.* Ex. "You may have soup or salad with that." In this book, we mean "or" in the inclusive sense. Also called a **Disjunction.**

Premise – Any statement that is used to try to convince someone that a conclusion is true.

Question – A sentence that asks without providing an answer. Not a statement. Cannot be a premise or a conclusion.

Rational reconstruction – This is what you end up with when you take someone else's sloppy argument and turn it into clear statements that you can analyze. This may mean taking any commands, questions, and exclamations that are intended as premises and conclusions and turning them into statements, and adding any implied statements. Present the argument in its best light. Rational reconstruction is generally a polite thing to do. At the end, the other person should be able to say, "Yeah, that's what I meant."

Simple Statement – Statements that have no logical connectives in them.

Sound – A valid argument that has all true premises. A deductive argument you can believe.

Statement – A sentence that can be true or false (has "truth value").

Strong – An inductive argument in which the premises would offer very good support for the conclusion if they were true, although they cannot guarantee it. The premises might be false, though.

Syllogism – An argument with exactly two premises and a conclusion. Not all arguments are syllogism – arguments can have several premises, or one, or none. However, all arguments have exactly one conclusion.

Unsound – An argument that is either invalid, or has at least one false premise, or both.

Valid – An argument is valid when it is impossible for the premises to be true and the conclusion false.

Weak – An inductive argument in which the premises do not offer good support for the conclusion, even if they were true (which they might or might not be). Weak arguments are not very good.

Index

Made in United States
Orlando, FL
11 April 2022